Hidden Messages
Decoding the Complex World of Micro-Expressions

Table of Contents

Chapter 1. Introduction

Dive into the fascinating world of nonverbal communication with our Special Report, "Hidden Messages: Decoding the Complex World of Micro-Expressions." This comprehensive investigation not only takes a straightforward, accessible walk through the increasingly recognized field of psychology and its subtle intricacies but also swiftly leads you into the heart of human interactions. Learn to unravel those quick, almost imperceptible facial movements that reveal what words often strive to conceal. This enlightening report is a must-have for everyone - from the eager enthusiast to the seasoned professional. With engaging content framed in an easy-to-grasp style, our report promises to equip you with the key to unlock profound depths of understanding and empathy. Take the reins and transform your everyday communications from the ordinary to the extraordinary! Secure your copy of the Special Report today, and start unveiling the hidden messages that surround us all!

Chapter 2. The Science of Micro-Expressions: An Overview

The human face, a canvas of expression, expresses numerous emotions. These emotions, whether prominently displayed or subtly presented, hold key information about our internal state. The study of these facial expressions, particularly the subtle, almost unperceivable ones, presents a remarkable science in itself, the science of micro-expressions.

2.1. Understanding Micro-Expressions

Micro-expressions, fleeting, involuntary facial expressions, last no more than a fraction of a second, typically 1/25 to 1/15 of a second. They are often the byproduct of powerful, intense emotions that an individual is determined and conscious to hide. However, as they are automatic and largely uncontrollable, they offer an unguarded, authentic glimpse into an individual's emotional state.

2.2. The Relevance of Micro-Expressions

Micro-expressions play a significant role in understanding the concealed layers of human emotions, bridging the gap between external presentation and internal feelings. They hold considerable value for a variety of professions, most notably in law enforcement, behavioral sciences, and therapeutic professions. They enable the interpretation of subconscious cues, often bypassed in regular communication, to unriddle veiled emotions.

2.3. Unveiling the Facial Coding System

In the late 1960s, American psychologist Paul Ekman developed the Facial Action Coding System (FACS), a comprehensive anatomical model of facial muscle movement. The FACS cataloged the activity of all possible facial muscles involved in presentable expressions, constituting a revolutionary step towards understanding the language of expressions.

2.4. The Seven Universal Micro-Expressions

Ekman's extensive research led to the identification of seven micro-expressions universally adopted, irrespective of culture or language. These expressions: happiness, sadness, surprise, fear, disgust, anger, and contempt are a part of the fundamental human instinct, deeply rooted in our evolution.

2.5. Deciphering Micro-Expressions

Micro-expressions are often transient and elusive. Hence, a trained eye is required to spot and interpret them accurately. Tools like high-speed cameras are employed in research environments to slow down and break up human expression, enabling a detailed study of the underlying micro-expressions.

2.6. The Cognitive Mechanisms behind Micro-Expressions

Micro-expressions are believed to be the result of two battling mental processes: the conscious or unconscious urge to conceal a feeling and the involuntary leakage of that same emotion. This duality results from a clash between the limbic system, our emotional control center, and the cortex, responsible for controlling our expressive tendencies.

2.7. Significance of Micro-Expressions in Real-world Applications

Micro-expressions offer significant practical benefits, particularly in professions dependent on human interaction. They are extensively used in lie detection, counseling, negotiation, and even sales. Understanding micro-expressions can refine interpersonal interactions by promoting empathic understanding and facilitating honest communication.

2.8. Challenges and Limitations

Despite the increasing acceptance of micro-expression analysis, the field is not without its limitations. One of the key limitations is the difficulty in accurately spotting and interpreting micro-expressions. Misinterpretation can sometimes lead to understanding a person's intent or emotion incorrectly.

2.9. Looking Ahead

The study and understanding of micro-expressions holds immense potential. As technology evolves and our comprehension of the brain deepens, the field of micro-expressions is poised for remarkable growth. Upcoming advancements, like artificial intelligence-driven recognition software, promise to transform the science and unlock new doors to our understanding of human emotion.

In summary, the science of micro-expressions unlocks the door to a deeper understanding of human emotions. By mastering this fascinating skill, one can considerably improve their interpersonal communication and foster a better understanding of humanity's emotional language.

Chapter 3. Decoding Facial Cues: A Deep Dive

For many years, the science of understanding facial expressions and nonverbal cues remained restricted. Now more than ever, it's recognized as an integral part of effective communication. This chapter seeks to dissect the breadth and depth of facial cues.

3.1. Understanding the Basis of Facial Cues

Facial cues are a form of nonverbal communication where information is conveyed through facial expressions. These expressions are often automatic responses that provide real-time feedback about a person's emotional state. They go beyond the spoken words, carrying a depth of meaning that, at times, words cannot capture entirely.

It can be traced back to Charles Darwin's seminal work, "The Expression of the Emotions in Man and Animals," where Darwin posited that facial expressions evolved to quickly communicate emotional states necessary for survival. This concept reinforces that by understanding what each expression conveys, it's possible to enhance interpersonal communication.

3.2. The Facial Action Coding System (FACS)

To decode facial cues accurately, you need to familiarize yourself with the Facial Action Coding System (FACS). Developed by Ekman and Friesen in the late '70s, this system has become the standard tool for identifying and classifying "Action Units" (AUs) or distinct muscle movements that create facial expressions.

FACS integrates over 10,000 possible combinations of AUs. Not every AU emanates an emotional connotation. However, the combination of various action units could express different emotions. For instance, an AU combination could suggest happiness or fear, disgust or joy.

3.3. Seven Fundamental Facial Expressions

Acknowledged universally, seven primary facial expressions reflect basic human emotions: Happiness, Sadness, Disgust, Fear, Anger, Surprise, and Contempt. Each comes with distinct features easily recognizable once you know what to look for.

For example, happiness visibly appears as relaxed eyes, cheeks rising, and a broad smile. Conversely, anger conveys with furrowed eyebrows, dilated nostrils, and tightened lips.

3.4. Micro-expressions and Their Importance

Micro-expressions are quick expressions, typically lasting 1/15 to 1/25 of a second. These fleeting expressions can be highly revealing, providing insight into someone's true emotional state even if they are trying to hide it.

Because micro-expressions occur involuntarily, they can reveal deception or help understand someone's feelings better. Trained observers who can pick up on these quick expressions will have a significant advantage in their interactions, from social encounters to professional settings.

3.5. The Art of Decoding Facial Cues

Since individuals cannot readily control their facial expressions - especially micro-expressions- understanding them becomes crucial. A few broad areas to note include:

- Eyes: A lot could be unveiled by paying attention to the direction of someone's gaze, pupils' size, brow movements, and the frequency of blinking.

- Mouth: The shape of the mouth can be very revealing. A genuine smile, often known as a Duchenne smile, activates certain facial muscles that cannot be consciously controlled.

- Other Features: Other areas, such as the nose, forehead, and chin, can provide supplemental cues, although they are often overlooked.

3.6. Interpreting Facial Cues in Context

While individual expressions can provide valuable clues about a person's feelings, they must be interpreted in their context. Cultural differences, personal tendencies, and ambient circumstances should be considered to avoid misinterpretation. Hence, the assessment of nonverbal cues needs to be layered and multidimensional.

Using the insights of nonverbal cues might seem complex and requires practice but once understood, it can add a new dimension to communication. Ultimately, learning to decode facial cues can significantly impact understanding others, promoting empathy, and effective communication. Therefore, it's a skill worth investing both time and effort into acquiring.

Keep in mind that this decoding is an art more than a precise science and individual differences should always be taken into account.

While significant strides have been made towards understanding and classifying facial cues, there's still plenty of room for individual interpretations and unique variations.

In conclusion, the facial expressions are a window into the soul. By unlocking the ability to read these, we invite the chance to foster deeper connections with ourselves and those around us. The skill to decode facial cues engenders a richness in our interactions and narratives, paving the way to an all-round enriched life.

Chapter 4. Micro-Expressions Across Cultures: A Comparative Analysis

In the diverse spectrum of human interaction, micro-expressions hold a significant place as universal indicators of genuine emotion. These fleeting, involuntary facial movements often escape conscious control and reveal what our words might conceal. The exploration of micro-expressions across different cultures offers insights into both the universality and cross-cultural variance of human expressions.

4.1. The Universality of Micro-Expressions

Psychologist Paul Ekman, best known for his work on the universality of facial expressions, has identified seven emotions - happiness, sadness, anger, surprise, fear, disgust, and contempt - that consistently correspond to specific facial micro-expressions across cultures. This implies that regardless of social, ethnic, or geographical background, humans exhibit universal micro-expressions reflecting these basic emotions. For instance, the crinkling of the eyes is a universal indicator of genuine happiness, while the contraction of the eyebrows is globally a sign of anger.

However, while these universal micro-expressions exist, cultural norms and practices may influence their interpretation and the context in which these expressions occur.

4.2. Interpretation Variations

Culture plays a substantial role in the ascription of meaning to micro-expressions. While the physiological manifestation of emotions may be universal, the interpretation can be culturally-specific at times.

Eastern cultures, for example, largely emphasize public harmony and collective welfare. As such, individuals may suppress certain emotions or micro-expressions, like anger or disgust, that might disrupt societal balance. Contrastingly, Western cultures, which focus on individualism, may interpret these suppressed or muted expressions differently, potentially misreading the emotional state of the individual.

4.3. Effect of Cultural Display Rules

Cultural display rules, which dictate when and how emotions should be exhibited based on our cultural upbringing, greatly influence the way we control and modify our facial expressions. These unspoken rules might cause what Ekman coined as "emotion work," where an individual refines or suppresses certain micro-expressions to match societal expectations. This often leads to 'masked' or 'false' micro-expressions.

Understanding these display rules becomes crucial when interpreting micro-expressions in intercultural interactions, as failing to do so can potentially lead to miscommunication and misunderstandings.

4.4. The Role of Acculturation

Acculturation, the adaptation process when individuals adopt traits from another culture, affects micro-expression processing abilities, with implications for cross-cultural communication. Research suggests that individuals who are more acquainted with a second culture become better at identifying and interpreting micro-expressions from individuals of that culture. Thus, acculturation plays a pivotal role in enhancing the accurate interpretation of micro-expressions across cultures.

4.5. Developing Micro-Expression Literacy

Enhancing one's literacy in reading micro-expressions, referred to as 'micro-expression literacy', is a skill with broad application. Notably, it assists in detecting deceit, understanding unspoken sentiments, and promoting healthier cross-cultural communications by fostering empathy. Learning resources, both theoretical and practical, can support this development, though it requires consistent practice due to the short duration and subtle nature of these expressions.

Micro-expressions encompass a fascinating realm of non-verbal communication. Despite their universality, cultural influences on their interpretation and expression cannot be denied. Understanding these cultural nuances is critical for precise interpretation and fostering effective cross-cultural communication. As our world becomes increasingly interconnected, the role of micro-expression literacy in enhancing our understanding of each other is particularly salient. In this vital field of subtle interactions, everyone stands a chance to become more attuned to the silent language we all share.

Chapter 5. Emotional Intelligence and Micro-Expressions: The Connection

Before we delve deeply into the world of micro-expressions, one term demands our immediate attention - emotional intelligence. Akin to a key to understanding the complex dance of micro-expressions, emotional intelligence, often abbreviated as EI or EQ (Emotional Quotient), is the ability to identify, understand, and manage our emotions and those of others. Our journey through the connection between emotional intelligence and micro-expressions starts right here.

5.1. What is Emotional Intelligence?

Emotional intelligence entails five primary components, namely: self-awareness, self-regulation, social skills, empathy, and motivation.

Self-awareness: This principle revolves around the ability to recognize and understand personal moods, emotions, and drives, as well as their effect on others.

Self-regulation: Once we have perceived our feelings, the next step is to control or redirect them, especially when they are disruptive.

Social skills: Emotional intelligence also enables handling relationships judiciously and empathetically, including proficiency in managing social situations and interactions.

Empathy: Those with high emotional intelligence can understand the emotional makeup of other people, resulting in a greater level of compassion and connection.

Motivation: The final component is the internal drive to achieve, which gears towards the passion to work for reasons that go beyond material rewards.

5.2. Emotional Intelligence and Micro-Expressions: A Symbiotic Relationship

Now let us navigate towards understanding the profound relationship between Emotional Intelligence and Micro-Expressions.

Micro-expressions, fleeting automatic expressions that appear on an individual's face for a fraction of a second, incredibly reveal genuine emotions, which are typically concealed purposely or unconsciously. The capacity to accurately detect these quick-fire expressions can significantly augment emotional intelligence, creating a symbiotic relationship between the two.

With a high degree of EI, one can discern, appreciate, and harness the emotions reflected in micro-expressions, thereby increasing the richness and efficiency of interpersonal communication. Similarly, elaborate knowledge about micro-expressions further fosters emotional intelligence, producing a powerful synergy that is both intriguing and essential in the realm of human communications.

5.3. Micro-Expressions: The Invisible Facet of Communication

Micro-expressions, miniature replicas of human emotions, happen involuntarily as we react to various stimuli in our surroundings. Unlike normal facial expressions, these are extremely rapid, appearing and disappearing in as little as 1/25th of a second. These "micro" instances often reveal the most genuine emotions that one might be trying to conceal.

Research shows seven universal micro-expressions: joy, surprise, contempt, sadness, fear, disgust, and anger. The universal nature of these expressions implies that people from varied cultural backgrounds demonstrate them in a similar fashion. This characteristic further enhances the role of micro-expressions in augmenting emotional intelligence, enabling us to empathize with individuals from very different cultures or backgrounds.

5.4. Training Yourself to Detect Micro-Expressions

As the adage goes, "practice makes perfect," developing a keen eye for these micro-expressions is no different. The more you practice observing people in different contexts and mindfully noticing the subtler aspects of their facial expressions, the better you'll become at accurately interpreting their feelings.

User-friendly tools such as the Facial Action Coding System (FACS) might aid in this process. Devised by psychologists, this comprehensive tool serves as a manual to the visible effects of facial muscle movements, offering an analytical method for measuring and categorizing observable facial movements.

Despite the initial challenge, this newfound ability to read micro-expressions can bring considerable benefits to our personal and professional lives, truly transforming everyday communication into an intriguing journey of discovery.

5.5. Emotional Intelligence in Application: The Rewards

While the primary focus of our discussion is decoding micro-expressions, it is equally necessary to recognize how effectively applying emotional intelligence brings forth both personal and professional benefits.

Personal relationships flourish when underscored by emotional intelligence. Understanding and responding to the micro-expressions of loved ones can enhance connections, clearing paths for empathy, compassion, and openness.

In a professional setting, a manager competent in reading their team's micro-expressions will lead more effectively, fostering stronger relationships, enhancing teamwork, motivating employees, and thereby contributing to a positive workplace environment.

To conclude, understanding the connection between emotional intelligence and micro-expressions is not just an enlightening journey but a transformative one. This acquired skill of discerning 'hidden messages' can enhance our lives significantly, paving the way for better interpersonal connections, stronger bonds, and a heightened sense of empathy. Cultivate emotional intelligence, master the art of spotting micro-expressions, and watch your interpersonal communications transform from ordinary to extraordinary.

Chapter 6. Micro-Expressions in Our Everyday Life: Real World Applications

The importance of understanding the subtleties of human communication cannot be overstated. Amongst the myriad ways we speak without words is through micro-expressions, fleeting, almost invisible movements on the face that reveal a surplus of meaning. Whether at home, at the workplace, or in social settings, these rapid flickers of emotion are quietly at work, allowing us to gauge the emotional climates around us knowingly or unknowingly. In this chapter, we will delve into real-world scenarios where decoding micro-expressions can significantly profit all areas of our everyday lives.

6.1. Impact in Personal Relationships

Micro-expressions play a vital role in our personal lives. However, we might not even be aware of those fleeting glimpses of feelings that tell more about a personal situation than words can convey. Recognizing and interpreting these can help foster deeper understanding and empathy in relationships.

For instance, a slight tightening of your partner's mouth when discussing a touchy subject might reveal discomfort or disagreement. This could provide valuable insights into how to handle the conversation delicely.

Remember, the key hinges on observation and interpretation. You might confuse surprise with fear or anger with disgust if not adept in spotting the subtle differences in these expressions and their precise timings. Practice and patience bear fruits here.

6.2. Use in a Professional Setting

In the workplace, understanding micro-expressions can be instrumental to achieving professional goals. You might be pitching a new idea to your team or negotiating a crucial deal with a client. Detecting and correctly interpreting the flicker of skepticism or uncertainty in the accompanying micro-expressions can help you tailor your communication efficiently.

For example, if the client's eyebrows crinkle in the middle when you highlight certain terms of the agreement, you might deduce a wrinkle of worry or disagreement there. Responding appropriately, you can address the concern immediately and keep the negotiation process smooth.

Again, it is imperative to remember that harnessing the power of micro-expressions in a professional setting requires keen observation, disciplined practice, and a consolidated understanding of different facial muscle movements and their emotional connections.

6.3. Instances in Social Interactions

Apart from personal relationships and professional environments, social interactions also provide numerous opportunities for the practical application of understanding micro-expressions. Whether it's sensing a friend's hidden distress during a casual meet-up or picking up on the subtle disinterest of an acquaintance, these nuanced emotional clues can help navigate social situations skillfully.

Suppose you noticed the fleeting tightening of a friend's eyes when asked about their work. There could be a hint of worry, signaling that they might be facing professional difficulties. Expressing concern and offering support at this juncture can strengthen your friendship and provide comfort to the friend.

However, bear in mind the potential cultural differences that might affect the interpretation of micro-expressions. While the basic facial expressions are universally similar, cultural nuances and individual differences add layers of complexity to it.

6.4. Path to Mastery

Mastering the art of micro-expressions is a journey tailored for those ready to invest in understanding the depth and breadth of human emotions. Starting from observing and identifying basic emotional responses, you gradually advance to pick up subtle changes in facial expression.

Practicing with online tools, learning from experts, and continuously observing people in various life scenarios can help hone this skill. A word of caution, though - striving for mastery doesn't mean violation of personal spaces. Respect for individual boundaries is equally essential to responsibly utilize this psychological tool.

Understanding micro-expressions can be transformative, radically changing our perception of the world around us. With knowledge comes responsibility, and armed with the insight gained through decoding these hidden messages, we have the potential to improve our own lives and those of others.

Chapter 7. Tools and Techniques for Micro-Expression Recognition

Given the essential role micro-expressions play in our everyday communications, it's crucial to understand the tools and techniques that enable us to recognize and interpret them accurately. The art of reading micro-expressions is a rapidly evolving field, with new technologies and psychological insights continually expanding our understanding.

7.1. Facial Action Coding System

The Facial Action Coding System (FACS) is a widely recognized and extensively used method to identify and categorize facial movements. Developed by psychologists Ekman and Friesen, FACS categorizes all visible facial movements into Action Units (AUs) - discreet facial movements like raising the eyebrows or tightening the lips. With 46 AUs that can combine in countless ways, FACS provides a comprehensive manual to the physical manifestation of emotion on the human face.

FACS' greatest strength is its detailed taxonomy of facial actions, making it a valuable resource for recognizing micro-expressions. However, learning FACS is like learning a new language, often requiring hundreds of hours of study and practice to attain competency.

7.2. Subtle Expression Training Tool

The Subtle Expression Training Tool (SETT), another pioneering work by Dr. Ekman, builds on FACS by focusing specifically on the brief, fleeting, and often partial facial expressions that constitute micro-expressions. SETT helps improve the recognition of seven primary emotions - happiness, sadness, anger, surprise, fear, disgust, and contentment - when displayed subtly. A big advantage is that SETT comes as a computer-based training, making it accessible and affordable for many.

7.3. Micro-Expression Training Tool

The Micro-Expression Training Tool (METT) is a natural complement to SETT, honing in on the rapid, less than half a second, facial expressions that flash across people's faces when they conceal or suppress their emotions. Like SETT, METT focuses on the core seven emotions and deploys computer-based training to help recognize these fleeting expressions, even when someone attempts to hide them.

7.4. Technology-Assisted Analysis

With the evolution of AI and machine learning, technology provides powerful tools to assist micro-expression recognition. Facial recognition software – such as OpenFace, Affectiva, and DeepFace – can detect and analyze detailed changes in the face down to the pixel level, at an astonishing frequency of hundreds of frames per second.

These tools not only provide objective, quantitative analysis that eliminates human bias efficiently but also hold a world of promise in adapting to real-world, real-time scenarios, given the sufficient input of diverse emotional expressions data.

7.5. Practical Techniques and Exercises

In the realm of practical human skills development, there are several effective techniques:

Practice makes perfect: Regular observation of people and their interactions - both in real life and through media like TV shows and films - can help attune you more to the subtleties of facial expressions.

Slow motion analysis: Watch video clips in slow motion to study facial expressions in detail - the micro-movements of the face will be more discernable with the reduced speed.

Photographic memory exercises: Viewing a series of faces for a few seconds each and then trying to identify the emotions displayed can help in sharpening recognition abilities.

Reflection and mindfulness: A surprising tool that can help with recognizing others' micro-expressions is becoming aware of your own. Practicing mindfulness can help become familiar with the sensations that accompany your own emotions, providing a reference point to understand others' feelings.

In conclusion, recognizing micro-expressions is an amalgamation of theoretical understanding, rigorous practice, and the judicious use of technology. It is a learned skill that can be significantly improved upon over time, making it an essential tool for anyone aiming to enhance their understanding and empathy in interpersonal communication. By integrating the toolset elaborated in this chapter, we can develop a heightened sense of awareness and responsiveness that can enrich our everyday interactions, bringing us a step closer to deciphering the underlying emotions and intentions in the fleeting expressions that cross human faces every day.

Chapter 8. Micro-Expressions in Professional Settings: An Inside View

The world of professional settings, dens of intrigue brimming with nuanced non-verbal expressions, is home to an intricate web of micro-expressions. These brief and typically unnoticed facial expressions frequently communicate meaningful, substantial information about a person's emotional state and intentions.

8.1. Why Micro-Expressions Matter

Micro-expressions are characterized by their brevity, often occurring in as little as 1/15 to 1/25 of a second. By contrast, typical facial expressions last around 1-4 seconds, marking a significant difference. This fleeting nature often makes micro-expressions go unnoticed, despite the depth of detail they can offer regarding emotional information.

At work, where professional conduct takes center stage, people often restrict their display of emotions. Regardless, human nature ensures the occurrence of emotional reactions, which naturally find an outlet - the face. Through these seemingly involuntary and subtle face movements, emotions such as disgust, happiness, fear, surprise, anger, sadness, and contempt are discernible. Mastering this language can be decisive in enhanced understanding, interaction, negotiations, or even conflict resolution, positioning improved non-verbal communication as an indispensable tool in the corporate world.

8.2. Recognizing Micro-Expressions

The study of Facial Action Coding System (FACS) offers an exhaustive methodology for identifying nearly any conceivable facial expression, placing importance on individual facial muscles or 'action units.' These 'action units' reflect distinct emotions, including those previously mentioned. An adept understanding of FACS will aid in recognizing and interpreting these micro-expressions.

While detecting micro-expressions can seem daunting, it is achievable with training and practice. Remember, just as verbal communication skills require time and effort to refine, so does reading micro-expressions. To begin, one really effective way is to observe others and pay attention to their subtle facial movements during interactions, especially high-stake discussions. Watching video footage with focus on frame-by-frame analysis of facial changes during emotional events can also be beneficial. Gradually, it becomes easier to recognize these transient facial movements in real-time scenarios.

8.3. Practical Application of Reading Micro-Expressions in Professional Settings

In the corporate world, the ability to accurately read micro-expressions opens up an arena of opportunities. It refines an individual's emotional awareness of colleagues, potential business partners, clients, or teams - a crucial cornerstone of emotional intelligence. Equipped with this comprehension, one can accordingly adapt their interactions to foster comfortable, productive relationships.

For instance, someone who has mastered recognizing disgust or contempt can gauge the true reaction colleagues or business partners have towards proposals, regardless of any uttered polite disagreements. On the other side, spotting genuine happiness and surprise could serve as an affirmation of decisions and ideas gaining traction.

In sales or negotiations, reading the potential client's positive or negative micro-expressions provides critical feedback on the pitch's effectiveness. Interpreting cues of interest, annoyance, or boredom can help the negotiator tailor the proceedings to ensure success. In team settings, leaders can positively use these reading capabilities to nurture a conducive work environment, identifying and promptly addressing any brewing conflict.

8.4. Overcoming Challenges in Recognizing Micro-Expressions

Deceptively simple as it may sound, decoding micro-expressions can be challenging. For starters, cultural variation in facial expressions may present a stumbling block. Although primary emotions are universal, they can be influenced by cultural norms. Understanding these cultural differences in the interpretation of emotions can assist in accurate decoding.

Additionally, as humans, we possess the natural ability to conceal our emotions or 'put on a face.' The intention to conceal real emotions can make it much harder to interpret micro-expressions, as these can be subtle and quick.

In summary, micro-expressions are a gateway to a deeper understanding of others' emotions, with a pivotal role in shaping impactful interpersonal communications, professional relationships, and successful negotiations. Decoding them enhances emotional intelligence, a cornerstone of productive work environments. By investing focused effort in understanding and identifying these expressions, individuals can transform professional communications from simple verbal relay of facts into an engaging ebb and flow of human connection. This formidable tool, in essence, offers an inside view into the hidden emotional world of your professional settings, opening up a whole new frontier of understanding, empathy, and connection.

Chapter 9. Impact of Micro-Expressions on Interpersonal Relationships

Understanding the silent dialogues that take place during every human interaction begins by decoding micro-expressions. Shedding light on these fleeting, almost invisible facial movements, allows us to delve deeper into the impact of these micro-expressions on interpersonal relationships. Fundamentally, they provide silent hints to our emotions, thoughts, and intentions, influencing our connections with individuals around us.

9.1. The Basis of Micro-Expression

A key source of interpersonal communication, micro-expressions are involuntary, brief emotional responses that flash across our faces almost without detection. Lasting no longer than one-fifteenth of a second, these momentary facial expressions reveal the emotional valence of an individual, and sometimes, their hidden feelings.

Insights from research conducted by Paul Ekman, a psychologist and pioneer in the study of emotions, demonstrates that these micro-expressions are universal. They occur across different cultures, indicating the same set of core emotions: happiness, sadness, anger, surprise, fear, disgust, and contempt.

9.2. Understanding Emotional Leakage

Emotional leakage is a concept closely intertwined with micro-expressions. It refers to the occurrences where our true feelings 'leak out' in the form of micro-expressions, despite our intentional attempts to camouflage or control them. Such instances can offer invaluable insight into a person's true state of mind during conversations or interactions.

9.3. Detecting Deception

Micro-expressions can serve as valuable tools for unmasking deception. Suppressing true emotions causes a conflict between felt and displayed emotions, producing incongruent micro-expressions. By learning to identify and interpret these subtle cues, a more accurate perception of the other's authentic feelings or potentially deceptive behavior might be gained.

9.4. Micro-Expressions and Empathy

Empathy, a necessary component in healthy relationships, finds a natural ally in the ability to read micro-expressions. An accurate comprehension of micro-expressions equips an individual with the means to understand the emotional experiences of other persons better, hence fostering heightened empathy.

Conversely, missed or misinterpreted micro-expressions could result in misunderstanding or conflicts, highlighting the essential role of micro-expression comprehension in promoting healthier interpersonal relationships.

9.5. Impact on Personal Relationships

Micro-expressions can critically influence personal relationships. They can serve as indicators of a person's true feelings when their words seem dubious. Understanding these subtle cues helps validate the feelings of the other person, leading to the building of trust and mutual respect.

To illustrate, consider an instance where a friend suppresses their feelings of sadness to maintain a cheerful facade. By catching the fleeting micro-expression of sadness, one can gently steer the conversation in a supportive direction, validating their inner emotional experience.

9.6. Impact on Professional Relationships

In professional relationships, the ability to decode micro-expressions might lead to more effective communication and collaboration. This proves particularly useful in leadership positions, where understanding team dynamics is critical. Leaders who can interpret micro-expressions accurately can potentially anticipate and navigate interpersonal conflicts better, fostering a more harmonious working environment.

9.7. Training and Application

The challenging nature of detecting and interpreting micro-expressions might seem a daunting task at first. However, with consistent practice and training, one can significantly improve this skill. Utilizing scientifically validated tools and training programs enables individuals to enhance their understanding and use of micro-expressions.

In conclusion, while it is clear that the subtle nuances of micro-expressions have far-reaching impacts on interpersonal relationships, it involves a level of emotional intelligence that comes with considerable practice. By honing these skills, we are able to foster more authentic, empathetic, and ultimately, more meaningful relationships, embellishing our social fabric's integrity and understanding.

Chapter 10. Pitfalls and Misinterpretations in Reading Micro-Expressions

Reading micro-expressions is an art that requires careful observation, practice, and understanding. Unfortunately, many pitfalls and misinterpretations can occur along the way, obscuring the clarity of the message being conveyed. This section will help you navigate these challenges, enabling you to deepen your understanding and improve your accuracy in interpreting micro-expressions.

10.1. Understanding Micro-Expressions and Their Variations

Micro-expressions are fleeting, usually lasting only a fraction of a second, but they speak volumes about our emotions. These quick, involuntary facial movements are subtle, and understanding them requires a measure of localizing even the smallest shifts in an individual's facial muscles. Because they are so quick and often suppressed, they can easily go unnoticed by the untrained observer. Moreover, they can sometimes be confused with general facial movements or expressions that have completely different implications.

One common pitfall is failing to recognize that micro-expressions differ across cultures. What might indicate anger in one culture might be a sign of annoyance or frustration in another. Learning to read micro-expressions should also involve learning about the various cultural, social, and personal factors that can influence facial expressions.

10.2. The Role of Context

Another common pitfall is ignoring the context in which the micro-expression occurs. Micro-expressions are not standalone signs that can be read in isolation; they are sense-making tools firmly rooted in context.

Observing a particular micro-expression doesn't implicitly reveal the entire emotional state of an individual. It is essential to consider what preceded the emotional response, the current situation, and the potential future implications. Misinterpretations often arise when readers take an observed micro-expression at face value without considering the context in which it is displayed.

10.3. The Pitfall of Projection

The pitfall of projection is also a significant challenge in accurately reading micro-expressions. This concept includes our inherent bias, where we interpret other's micro-expressions based on our own emotional states and experiences.

We often unconsciously project our emotions onto others, which can lead to misinterpretation of what their expressions really mean. For instance, if we are feeling stress or anxiety, we may perceive negative emotions in others' micro-expressions, even when they are not present.

10.4. Misinterpretation due to Limited Training or Practice

Without regular practice and training, it can be easy to miss, misread, or wrongly interpret micro-expressions. It's worth noting that no one is perfect at reading micro-expressions. Even the most trained and experienced readers make errors. Thus, it is essential to continuously learn, practice, and refine your interpretive skills.

10.5. Handling Incongruence and Mixed Signals

Incongruence between verbal communication and micro-expressions often leads to confusion. When words conflict with facial expressions, it is crucial to exercise caution in interpretation. However, this is not to suggest that the verbal message is false and the non-verbal is true. The incongruence could be due to cultural differences, social norms, or the individual masking their true feelings.

10.6. Understanding Emotional Ambiguity

Sometimes, the same facial movements may be linked to different emotions, leading to misinterpretation. For instance, the emotion of fear might resemble surprise due to some overlapping facial cues. This poses a challenge since the interpretation of micro-expressions depends on understanding the nuances that differentiate these similar expressions.

In conclusion, reading and accurately interpreting micro-expressions is a complex process, fraught with numerous pitfalls and potential misinterpretations. Understanding these challenges and practicing with intention and awareness can significantly enhance your ability to communicate and connect with people around you. By learning about the possible pitfalls and misconceptions and how to avoid them, you can develop more effective interpersonal skills and an enhanced understanding of human communication.

Chapter 11. The Future of Micro-Expression Research: Towards a More Empathetic World

As we stand today, at the precipice of advancing our understanding of microexpressions, we find ourselves peering into the future of a more empathetic world. A world where we understand not just the words spoken, but also the unvoiced emotions behind fleeting facial movements.

11.1. A New Era for Microexpression Research

Our journey starts with the dawn of a new age of microexpression research. In the past, research was hindered by the limitations of human observational capacity. However, with the development of sophisticated facial recognition technology, we have an exciting new avenue opening for more accurate and detailed data collection.

Imagine video technology capturing every minute twitch of the facial muscle, correlating it with a spectrum of emotions in real-time. Artificial Intelligence systems can help parse terabytes of raw data and present insightful findings about nuanced human emotions. Nonverbal communication, once an enigma, is set to evolve into a complex but tangible subject of study.

11.2. Empathy at the Heart of Technological Advancements

We live in a digital age, where most of our interactions are online, often lacking the subtlety and depth of face-to-face conversations. Technology, ironically, stands at the helm of an empathy revolution, ready to bridge this gap.

Virtual reality (VR) has already started simulating realistic human interactions with emotionally responsive avatars. University laboratories worldwide are exploring how VR and augmented reality (AR) could be deployed in microexpression training programs. These technologies could help psychologists, consultants, HR professionals, and many others be more attuned to microexpressions, thereby honing their empathetic skills.

11.3. The Power of Machine Learning

Machine learning offers an attractive prospect in making sense of the complexity inherent in human expressions. It employs sophisticated algorithms to learn from the data it processes, enhancing its accuracy over time. This approach has the potential to greatly improve our understanding of complex microexpressions and their relationship with the internal emotional state.

Machine learning models could eventually surpass the capabilities of the human eye and memory retention, picking up on the most minute of changes, and correlating these changes with specific emotions. This groundbreaking technology could revolutionize our comprehension of nonverbal communication, leading to fascinating new discoveries in the field.

11.4. Harnessing the Promise of AI Assistants

Imagine a day when we have our personal AI assistants trained to read our emotions through our microexpressions. How much more efficient and empathetic our interactions could be! Whether it's detecting anxiety during a medical examination or understanding dissatisfaction in a business meeting, the applications are immense.

Such technology will not usurp the human element but act as an aid, enhancing our innate capacities. It is about integrating the richness of human empathy with the precision of technology.

11.5. Challenges on the Horizon

Despite its immense promise, the journey ahead is not without its challenges. Ethics becomes a vital consideration. While we strive to understand each other better, we must ensure to respect individual privacy rights. Usage of such technology must be under the premise of voluntary participation and informed consent.

Further, the complexity of psychological mapping, due to human emotion's fluid nature, cannot be overlooked. More extensive research is needed to shed light on the gray areas and refine our understanding. Globally accepted standards must be established for the interpretation of facial microexpression data.

11.6. Into A More Empathetic Future

We are standing on the cusp of the future, a future where nuanced understanding of emotions becomes a widespread norm. As technology and human understanding converge, this journey of decoding microexpressions is leading us towards a more empathetic world. While myriad complexities wait to be conquered, the immense potential for human understanding and connection keeps us resolute on this path.

Progress in the understanding of microexpressions might start as slow ripples in a vast ocean, but it promises a tsunamic shift in how we communicate and connect. While it is still an evolving field of study, the implication of comprehensive understanding is profound—promising not just individual growth, but the potential for humanity as a whole to move towards a harmonious future.